National Geographic School Publishing

Recycling Rules!

PIONEER EDITION

By Barbara Keeler

CONTENTS

Recycling Rules!

By Barbara Keeler

In the U.S., a family of four can throw out 2,907 kilograms (6,409 pounds) of trash each year. That's about as much as 115 third graders weigh! Trash can pollute the planet and hurt wildlife. The good news is that some trash can be recycled. Recycling means less trash for the Earth.

Recycling Resources

W hy should we **recycle**? It takes lots of resources to make new things. When we recycle, Earth is not harmed to get new resources. Making new things also takes lots of energy. Recycling saves energy.

Stripped Bare. Miners have stripped this forest land to mine **bauxite** ore.

Trashing the Earth

Trash is usually made up of solids, liquids, and gases. A lot of trash goes to **landfills**. Landfills can take up a lot of space. Think about an empty juice can. The metal can, a solid, takes up space even if it is squished. Any leftover liquid in the can takes up space, too. Even the air in the can, which is a gas, takes up space.

Trash Heap. Recycling can help keep some things out of landfills.

Recycling Glass

Glass is often recycled. Glass is sorted by color. Then it is crushed and melted to a liquid in a hot furnace.

The melted glass is blown into molds. It hardens back into a solid. It is used to make a bottle or jar.

Recycling one glass jar saves enough energy to light a 100-watt lightbulb for four hours.

Recycling Metals

What happens to a can when it's recycled? First, it goes to a recycling plant. Then, giant blades shred it. Next a huge furnace melts it from a solid to a liquid. This uses a lot of energy. But it does not use as much energy as melting new metal.

The liquid metal cools to a solid. The solid metal is used to make new cans or other metal products.

Recycling Plastic

Plastic can last for hundreds of years. So it's a good idea to reuse it! Recycled plastic can be used for a lot of things. Some carpet fiber is made from it. So are some clothes.

Plastic is hard to recycle. Why? Different plastics contain different materials. They have different properties. They melt at different temperatures. This makes it hard to recycle them.

When it is recycled, most trash changes from solid to liquid and then back to solid. Sometimes gases are added during the recycling process. When gas is added to liquid plastic, it makes plastic foam. Plastic foam is used for insulated cups.

We can recycle trash by changing its state. Recycling helps the environment.

Tree Musketeers

The city of El Segundo, California, picks up and recycles plastic. Brook Church remembers when the city had no recycling program. That's why he started one at age 12. He, his ten-year-old sister, and some friends were in a group. It was called Tree Musketeers.

Making a Difference. Tree Musketeers helped residents recycle until the city set up a program.

The Tree Musketeers set up huge bins. People dropped off items to recycle. Parents drove the solids to a recycling center.

Years passed. People wanted recycling picked up from their homes. Tree Musketeers asked the city to do this, but the city said no. So Tree Musketeers found another way.

Success!

Tree Musketeers called a waste hauler to pick up **recyclables**. But using the hauler cost money. The program cost $6.00 a month. People signed up for it.

For years, Tree Musketeers collected money for the waste hauler. Finally, the city took over. It started picking up recyclables at people's homes for free.

Recycling Everywhere

Now many cities have curbside recycling.
Kids are making recycling part of their lives.

The kids in Santa Rosa Beach, Florida helped their town. They worked to get more blue bags for the blue bag program. People put recyclables into blue bags. The bags are picked up with the trash. At the landfill, workers take the blue bags out. They recycle what is in them.

Gwen Wright's 1st-grade class at Butler Elementary helped out. Her class had a petition asking stores to sell blue bags. They got 239 students to sign. Some stores began to sell bags. The county then gave out some free bags.

Ella Robinson lives in Santa Rosa Beach, Florida. **She is learning not to make solid trash.** This way, no energy is used to melt solids for recycling. Ella takes her own cloth napkin to school. She washes her own dishes there. When she shops with her grandmother, they take their own shopping bags.

These kids and many others are making recycling a bigger part of their communities.

Watching Your Waste: The 4 Rs

Here are a few ways you can help reduce waste.

REDUCE

Buy things with no or little packaging.

Take your own bags to the store.

Take your own containers for leftovers.

Buy reusable, not disposable (dishes, napkins, towels, dishcloths).

REUSE

Reuse containers.

Write notes on used paper.

Buy used things. Repair, sell, or give away old things.

RECYCLE

Look for recycling bins when you are out.

Write to companies who make plastic containers. Ask them to put symbols on lids so recycling centers will take them.

RECLAIM

Buy products made from recycled materials.

Buy products with recycled packaging and containers.

Wordwise

bauxite: the ore from which aluminum is made

landfill: an area of land where trash is stored

recycle: make into new products

recyclables: things that can be made into new products

Clunkers
From the Road to the Recycler

Sometimes old cars aren't good for driving anymore. These cars are sometimes called clunkers. Some of them are sold for scrap. Many of their parts are recycled.

The car parts shown here can be used again.

windows

windshield

front end

wheel

body panels

back end

When a clunker is sold for scrap, first the liquids, like oil and gas, are removed. Some are recycled.

Next, the car is often flattened. Then it is crushed. The parts are shredded. The metals are taken out and melted down. They are formed into other products.

What happens to the tires? Many landfills will not take tires. They take up too much space. They don't break down easily. Good tires are used for other cars. Some are used in other ways, like for building walls in floods. Others are recycled. They may even be cut up into other things, like sandals!

Recycling Rules!

Recycling matters! Answer these questions to see what you have learned.

1 List three reasons to recycle.

2 How is metal recycled?

3 Why is plastic harder to recycle than metal?

4 What did Tree Musketeers do for El Segundo?

5 What happens to some old cars that are taken off the road?

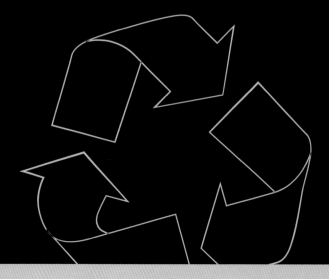